bosch

bosch

Text by
JOSEPH-EMILE MULLER

LEON AMIEL · PUBLISHER
NEW YORK

Published by
LEON AMIEL • PUBLISHER
NEW YORK
ISBN 0-8148-0640-6
Printed in the United States of America

ments that mention his name do not throw much light on the question. They do tell us, however, that in 1504 a *Last Judgment* was commissioned by Philip the Fair, prince of the Netherlands, thus giving us an idea of his reputation. Did Bosch also paint for himself? He could well have done so, for his marriage (around 1480) to Aleid van de Meervenne, a wealthy aristocrat, freed him from material needs so that he did not have to accept commissions. However, it may be, the originality of his art presupposes considerable freedom.

Bosch's work is as unusual as it is disconcerting. At every moment the viewer is confronted with beings, objects and situations that strain the limits of the imagination. Often we are led to ask questions that cannot be answered in a satisfactory way. Different writers have put forward hypotheses that more often than not show less of an artistic sensibility than a fondness for erudite dissertation. Although at first glance some may appear attractive, an attentive examination of the works themselves makes it difficult to accept all of their points without reserve. For example, Jacques Combe writes that "the thought of the painter seems to be in almost constant accord with that of the mystics of the fourteenth century, in particular with Ruysbroek's." In addition, Bosch's art reflects the alchemistic doctrine, "an esoteric philosophy that expresses itself in enigmas and frequently obscure symbols." In other words, in Bosch's work a hollow oak stands for "an emblem of the alchemists' furnace." A fish is "a symbol of sin and evil thoughts;" a bagpipe, "an obscene figure of carnal love;" an owl, "the symbol of those who prefer the night of sin and heresy to divine light." It is true that during the Middle Ages things were considered less in terms of themselves than as symbols of spiritual or moral ideas. Nonetheless, a bagpipe could certainly be perceived as a musical instrument, and a hollow tree could be found worthy of interest outside of any alchemistic considerations.

Another of Bosch's interpreters, Wilhelm Fraenger, believed he had detected in his work the symbolism of the heretical sect of the "Men of Free Spirit." However, it cannot be proved that this sect was active at Bois-le-Duc toward the end of the fifteenth century. Moreover, even if the artist used symbols belonging to this sect, does that necessarily mean that he was a member of it? One can illustrate a heresy without adopting it. How many novelists have their characters express ideas that they do not approve but which are used to define these characters? The fact that Bosch may have belonged to the Brotherhood of Notre-Dame also shows that he was not really so heretical, since this brotherhood had only religious aims, and its members came together for prayer and were enjoined to practice charity. Furthermore, it is not necessary to see in his art anything more than the response of a believer to certain circumstances.

Bosch worked at a time when the foundations of the medieval world were being shaken, and the Catholic church was confronted with ideas and trends that some saw as liberating, others as dangerous. Bosch was no doubt of the latter opinion. Around him he saw nothing but a world of sin, vice, madness, and depravity. It looked as if mankind were rushing toward its doom. Bosch's concern was to sound the alarm, to bring man back to the path of truth he had lost. How else can the passion and obstinacy with which he kept returning to this task be explained? We must be careful not to misinterpret his droll images. Bosch's purpose was not to amuse the viewer but to warn him, to save him.

It has been said that Bosch's style, which is at once cruel and refined, recalls the language of the preachers of that time, who also made use of sharp contrasts and, like Bosch, enjoyed evoking demons and other horrible, terrifying images. Nor should we forget that his epoch attributed powers to demons that are difficult for us to understand today. It has also been observed that proverbs and the popular theater might also have encouraged the painter to represent a certain character or scene. Which is to say that his art was undoubtedly less esoteric for his contemporaries than it is for us. The images they saw in his pictures expressed a mentality that must have been familiar to them. Yet it would be a mistake to think that Bosch simply translated into painting what others had expressed by different means. We must not underestimate his creative power nor his fertile imagination.

Where and how Bosch learned his art is not known. Prudence must be exercised in looking for predecessors who might have influenced him. Unquestionably Bosch was acquainted with the developments of Flemish art in the fifteenth century. He also must have consulted prints and books illustrated with miniatures or engravings. However, none of the relationships established between one of his pictures and an earlier work are convincing. Nor do they reveal anything of real importance, precisely because of Bosch's great originality, his ability to invent and innovate, and thus to remain outside the sphere of influence of his predecessors. It is worth recalling here that Bosch worked in a provincial milieu free of the weight of the great tradition, where it was difficult to maintain contact with the academic schools of Flanders.

As for Bosch's development as a painter, none of the thirty paintings now attributed to him bears a date. Sometimes one art historian will place at the beginning of his career a picture that, according to another, was done toward the end. Must we then renounce all attempts to draw up a chronological order? Charles de Tolnay has drawn up one, acceptable as a general outline, which we will use for our purposes here. However, we should not forget that we are dealing with an hypothesis and not an unquestionable certainty.

II   Even in the pictures supposedly executed before 1480, the unique characteristics of Bosch's style are obvious. Whether its subject matter is religious or profane, his painting is concerned with presenting more than just a spectacle; it seeks to impart a lesson. Sometimes the lesson is apparent at once. When we see a not especially reassuring doctor who is about to open the head of a fat, silly person with a knife, we have no difficulty understanding that the *Cure of Folly* (Prado, Madrid) shows how the credulous are deceived and exploited. In the *Seven Deadly Sins* (Prado, Madrid), the characters whom we see eating and drinking voraciously, as well as the woman who is putting on her coif in front of a mirror supplied by a treacherously helpful little devil, are easily recognizable as illustrations of gluttony and vanity. Nor is it difficult to understand the meaning of *The Epiphany* (Prado, Madrid) nor that of *Ecce Homo* (Staedel Institute, Frankfurt). *The Conjuror* (Municipal Museum, Saint-Germain-en-Laye) can be "read" easily as well, at least with regard to its overall meaning, for it also must be noted that the title refers to two characters: the prestidigitator who distracts the onlookers, and his accomplice who steals the purse of an old fool fascinated by the tricks of the illusionist. Without doubt Bosch is again warning the viewer about the dangers of credulity, a warning specifically addressed to those who are taken in by deceptive spectacles. However, some details in the picture are hard to interpret, and Bosch's interpreters provide different explanations for them.

The questions raised by *The Marriage at Cana* are more numerous and more fundamental. Different things appear enigmatic. Of course we immediately recognize Christ, the Virgin, the newly married couple, the guests and servants. But what about the figure in front of the buffet in the background who is holding a wand in his hand? Is he the major-domo directing the service? Or a magician? And what is the boar's head spitting that a waiter carries in on a platter? Is it poison? Is it a flame that shoots out of the swan's beak on the second plate? And what is the reason for the poison and the lightning-like flame? Why are the cherubims above the capitals animated; why does one threaten to shoot an arrow at another who has taken refuge in a hole in the wall? Does a detail like this simply bear witness to Bosch's humor which, according to Léo van Puyvelde, plays such an important role in his work? Can we see it as a reflection of the customs of the period which, in the theater, church sermons, and even processions, found it natural to blend the serious with the amusing, and religion with trivial jokes? Or should we rather follow the interpretation of Charles de Tolnay and Jacques Combe, who see nearly all the characters grouped around Christ in *The Marriage at Cana* as heretics delighting in the food and wine which has been poisoned by the magician's wand? However, a close look at the picture makes it difficult to maintain the viewpoint that most of the characters express only "heresy and the pleasure of the senses" or that the guests are "drinking and talking" (Jacques Combe). While it is true that a few of the guests (but no more than is normal at a wedding) are engaged in conversation, not one is delighting in the food (poisoned or not), and only a young man is drinking; his face, besides, expresses spiritual fervor more than it does sensual pleasure. To sum up, nothing could be more serious than the atmosphere of the wedding. The main charac-

riors show that Bosch was an attentive observer of the real world. He knows how to render the weight of a fabric, the elegance of drapery; he likes to diversify the play of folds, to make it more complex. He can also simplify it so as to make the forms more compact. Yet it would be incorrect to say that, by making the volumes "more unsubstantial," he gives the figures in *Ecce Homo* or the *Conjuror* a "transparent, floating aspect" that makes them look like "phantoms from a dream" (J. Combe). Moreover, the landscapes that we perceive in the *Crucifixion* (Brussels, Royal Museum of Fine Arts), in the *Epiphany,* as in a few episodes of the *Seven Deadly Sins,* and especially in the *Cure of Folly,* prove that the contours of the land and the enveloping light are living, deeply experienced realities for Bosch. Indeed, to such a degree that this aspect of his art is extremely modern, and thanks to it his painting is decidedly oriented toward the future.

III   Bosch's most original and captivating works, if not the most powerful, are the triptychs and separate panels that probably once were part of larger ensembles. It is believed that he painted them in his artistic maturity, approximately between 1480 and 1510.

One of these panels, *The Ship of Fools* (Louvre, Paris), shows a dozen figures drinking, singing, crying out, gesticulating. In the foreground, on the right, we see a monk; on the left, a nun. Their mouths, gaping with wonder, are directed toward a cake hanging from the mast by a rope. It is impossible to misinterpret this scene: what preoccupies the nun and the monk as well as their companions is immediate pleasure. In the intoxication of the moment they have forgotten that on this ship, which will soon sink, they are losing their souls while waiting to lose their lives.

The *Hay-Wain* (Prado, Madrid), a triptych, is likewise inspired by the theme of the appetites that lead men to their doom. In the middle of the central panel we see a farm wagon heavily loaded with hay drawn by a team of monsters; behind it trails a retinue including the pope, the emperor, and princes. On the mound of hay we see a pair of lovers as well as a young girl singing and a young man playing the lute. They do not see the bluish demon next to them playing a clarinette, nor a guardian angel addressing a desperate prayer to

mons, who look as if they were half-animal, half-human, seem extraordinarily real.

Bosch's ability to create monsters is demonstrated in other triptychs, especially the *Temptation of Saint Anthony* (National Museum, Lisbon). There is a rider whose torso resembles a bird's body with wings outstretched; for his head he has a thistle flower, and he is riding a horse whose belly consists of a jug. There are human bodies with pigs' heads; a cow whose hindquarters are connected with the head of a large fish; a fish armed with a sword and piece of breast-plate; featherless birds; a grossly enlarged rat and turtle; a kneeling man whose back is the roof of a peasant's house; a withered tree in the hollow trunk of which a woman's head can be seen bowed over a swaddled child; the bark of the tree is shaped like a shoulder, an arm and a hand, with the branches as the fingers—these are some of the unusual creatures or things that Bosch portrays around Saint Anthony, next to men and women whose aspect is less disconcerting, if not more intelligible. A nightmarish light bathes the picture, in the center of which fantastic, partly dilapidated buildings rise up. In the background houses are burning, throwing a yellow and red glow against a nocturnal sky that demons, seated on an egg, a fish or flying boats, are crossing. To illustrate the various aspects that the demons assume in order to harass and torment Saint Anthony, no one has ever painted a spectacle that is more surrealistic and at the same time more probable.

A third triptych is devoted to the *Last Judgment* (Academy of Fine Arts, Vienna). However, today it is accepted that this triptych is not an original work by Bosch, but a copy that one of his disciples did after a painting that has not survived. Thus it is interesting more from an iconographical than from a formal viewpoint. In contrast to the almost idyllic peace of the earthly paradise portrayed on the left panel, the central panel shows us the effects of the Last Judgment. Only a small part of heaven is reserved for Christ, for the saints who adore Him, and for the angels blowing their trumpets. All the rest belongs to the kingdom of darkness, to the conflagrations setting the world ablaze, and to hell, where the damned are tortured by horrible demons. One is roasted in a stove, another is impaled, a third is crushed between two millstones, and a fourth is shut up in a barrel full of toads while a monster spits flames at his face.

On the right panel, Satan himself is enthroned at the entrance to his domain. With terrifying looks, a ferocious maw, a fire of live coals for a stomach, he waits for the damned who are being brought to him by devils even more appalling than those in the center panel. By forming such a total contrast with the paradisiac calm that surrounds Adam and Eve, this evocation of hell and this landscape of doom naturally tend to emphasize how much humanity must suffer for its sins.

At first glance, there would seem to be less pessimism in the *Garden of Earthly Delights* (Prado, Madrid). The left panel depicts Adam and Eve, but this time there is no serpent and they are not driven out of paradise. Very modest, Eve rises uncertainly to her feet, and her Creator holds her nicely by the hand to introduce her to Adam, who looks at her with surprise. Around them, distributed over almost the entire surface of the panel, there are trees, plants, flowers, a pond, and animals, from the lizard to the giraffe, from the bird to the elephant. Not surprisingly, there are also fabulous beasts: a unicorn, a sort of dog with two legs, a bird with three necks and three beaks. Most of these animals live together in peace. But here is a mouse with a cat's teeth, a frog caught in a bird's beak, a lion that has killed a roebuck . . . The Fountain of Youth is a construction in which the memories of plants and crustaceans are merged. Its complex regularity and strict symmetry make it look like a creation of man rather than a product of nature. Rising exactly above the middle of the composition, it depicts a vertical image that extends the vertical figure of the Creator, whose cloak, also matches the pink color of the fountain.

The springlike colors of the left panel may also be seen in the center one, and the light is imbued with the same serene quality. Are we still in paradise? Bosch makes abundant use of flowers and fruit (including large, succulent strawberries). There are also many animals and especially human beings who, in general, are completely nude. But whether he shows men or women with light or dark skins, the bodies are always svelte and graceful. Thus the artist is able to present his figures in very free positions, without the image becom-

(Similar structures can be seen in front of the horizon on the left panel.) In the group of nudes Bosch bears witness to his inexhaustible imaginative powers, just as in these bizarre, constructions that rise up from the ground, emphasizing the unreality of life in this garden of earthly delights, he shows his tremendous gift for dreamlike fantasy.

But is man able to stay in this paradise? The panel on the right provides the answer: once again, the conclusion of life is hell. This version of hell is perhaps less terrifying than the one in the *Last Judgment* in Vienna, but in it the devils nonetheless continue to torture the damned. Astounding things are again to be found in the kingdom of demons: a man with the head of a bird who swallows fishermen and evacuates them like excrement; a sharp, pointed knife that aggressively thrusts its way between two large ears pierced with an arrow; a man whose legs are the trunks of a hollow tree, whose body is the shell of a broken egg housing an inn, and whose head is covered with a millstone on which a bagpipe rests. Couples move in a circle around this bagpipe, each couple consisting of a fisherman and an oddly attired demon. The monstrous man can be perceived all the more clearly because his dimensions are larger than those of the other shapes, and because of his bright hues. This is not the only picture wherein Bosch gives certain objects a special emphasis by enlarging them, without taking into account the proportions that normally would be respected. But no doubt it is in this picture that he uses this method in the most expressive manner. He also uses it to emphasize a few musical instruments, such as a lute, a harp, a clarinette, and a hurdy-gurdy, which have become instruments of torture. The style employed to draw these objects, especially the hurdy-gurdy, confirms that in Bosch's work a pronounced realism can co-exist with the triumph of the freest irrationality.

In the *Creation of the World* (in grisaille), which one sees when the panels are closed, realism is unquestionably the strongest element. The presence of a few fantastic details does not keep one from admiring the surprisingly natural look of the vast, deep landscape. Seen from a bird's-eye view, the world seems to emerge from the waters surrounding it, impregnated with a pale light which is filtered through the clouds and touches it gently.

That in painting a landscape an artist should have been so sensitive to the effects of light is absolutely exceptional for the time. A similar spirit can be found only in Dürer's water-colors, not in his oil paintings.

Generally speaking, the *Garden of Earthly Delights* is characterized by the authority of its style. In the *Hay-Wain,* the rapid draftsman-ship is often approximate, and the bodies have little relief. The same cannot be said for the *Temptation of Saint Anthony.* Here the forms stand out more, and the tones are dis-tributed more intelligently. On darkened backgrounds reds and blues are held in bal-ance, giving the whole a more lucid articula-tion. In spite of the teeming of characters and animals, the *Garden of Earthly Delights* is also cleverly articulated thanks to a few geometric shapes and to the colors, which contrast with or echo each other. In addition, the drawing is more precise than ever, and, in spite of the softness of the modeling, the volumes are not lacking in mass. Whereas in Bosch's work human anatomy is usually presented in sum-mary fashion (the small size of his figures in-vites synthesis), animals, monsters, and ob-jects are defined in a rather detailed manner.

A slightly more realistic accent distinguishes the nudes in a *Last Judgment* of which only a fragment has survived (the Munich Pinakothek). There is a possibility that this was the picture that the painter executed in 1504 for Philip the Fair. Although they are still somewhat stiff, the bodies of those who have been brought to life have more fullness than usual; they seem less gothic. As for the demons who are lying in wait for them and leading them, they are characterized by a dynamism that can only be described as demonic. Endowed with wings and long, thin feathers, they readily describe impetuous movements, and their agitation appears all the more vivid against the dark background which contains only a few allusions to the external world.

In addition to the pictures which portray a plethora of miniscule creatures, Bosch created other works in which a single character of relatively important size occupies the foreground. We think of *Saint John at Patmos* (Gemäldegalerie, Dahlem-Berlin), *Saint Jerome Praying* (Museum of Fine Arts, Ghent), *Saint Christopher* (Madrid, private collection),

IV

or *John the Baptist in the Desert* (Lazaro-Galdiano Museum, Madrid). Behind each figure stretches a landscape with forests, meadows, lakes, mountains, and a bluish sky that grows gradually brighter as it approaches the horizon line. Once again, the artist sensitively portrays atmospheric effects and the variations of light.

A small demon, with a human head and insect's body, can be seen next to Saint John at Patmos. Not far from Saint Jerome there are a few curving, thorny plants; an owl has alighted on the withered branch of a hollow tree; the empty, perforated red skin of a round fruit floats on a stagnant pond. A fantastic, bristling plant also curves upward near John the Baptist; its fruits contain seeds that birds are pecking. However, there is less mystery in these works than in the triptychs. Clearly Bosch wishes to focus the viewer's attention on the saint, on his fervor, his prayer, and his meditation.

It is curious to note that, whereas Bosch created so many frail human beings, his John the Baptist is not at all emaciated by the ascetic life of the desert. On the contrary, we are impressed by his sturdy physique; if he stood upright, he would appear enormous. The feeling of calm that emanates from this picture is reinforced by the massive figure of the saint who meditates, stretched out on the ground, dressed in a large red cloak.

A similar impression can be found in the *Temptation of Saint Anthony* (Prado, Madrid) which it is believed Bosch painted toward the end of his career. Naturally Bosch brings his demons into play, but they do not swarm as they do in the Lisbon triptych and they look less annoying. Seated in such a way that his body resembles an unshakable block, his spirit withdrawn in meditation, his eyes fixed on something remote, the saint does not even seem to notice the rather small creatures that are trying to torment him. Furthermore, the viewer as well has difficulty perceiving them. His attention is more attracted by the ochers and greens that give the landscape a peaceful, familiar look.

In the foreground of the *Prodigal Son* (Boymans Museum, Rotterdam), a work which Bosch also probably executed toward the end of his life, we again see an isolated character. Earlier, on the closed panels of the *Hay-Wain,* he had painted a vagabond who in many ways resembles this figure. The two faces reveal similar experiences. Turned to the rear, they have an anxious, disappointed look. In addition, the bodies have the same stiffness. They are bowed, bent over in the same way, suggesting the hurried pace of someone who, menaced by a dog, tries to move forward on faltering legs. Each of the characters is carrying a stick in his hand and has a closed basket on his back. Each is also surrounded by ordinary reality, which, in the later picture, is pushed as far as the trivial. In front of the inn that the Prodigal Son leaves behind him, a sow and her piglets are leaning over a trough; next to the house, a man is urinating. In a word, the realistic tendency, which in Bosch's work is expressed only in a limited way, is here carried to an extreme, as it would be in the work of Pieter Bruegel and of other Dutch artists of the seventeenth century. Even the colors anticipate those that would often be used by the latter: the dominating hues are, in effect, beiges and grays. These colors tell us at once that we are in the presence of the monotonous, slightly dismal reality of everyday. But they also are suited to the disillusioned feelings of the vagabond.

Among the paintings that Bosch created early in his life, we have found a few, an *Epiphany,* an *Ecce Homo,* that have to do with the life of Christ. Still later, the Passion of Christ served as the subject for different pictures, and Bosch painted another *Epiphany* (Prado, Madrid) which is thought to be one of his last works.

It does not have much in common with the first version. This is not only because it is a triptych, the panels being reserved for the donors and their patrons, but also because the adoration of the wise men in the central panel does not have the affected character that it does in the earlier composition. Arranged with greater ease, the figures now all look in the direction of the Virgin, whereas before two were placed somewhat to the side and one directly faced the viewer. The thatched cottage is also seen under another angle: it "crowns" the scene, framing the characters and no longer simply rising behind them. In a word, its role, from a plastic point of view, is more meaningful. As for the landscape, which rises toward the sky, it has more depth and space. In addition to a few houses and a windmill, there are architectural structures which, although imaginary, seem possible. Through its tonality and atmosphere, this landscape rather resembles those that fill the background of the *Prodigal Son* and of the *Temptation of Saint Anthony* (Prado, Madrid).

Does this mean that the *Epiphany* is totally devoid of fantastic elements? Not at all, as can easily be judged from certain vestimentary details. Nor can it be said that the meaning of each thing is clearly revealed. For example, who is the half-naked man who can be seen at the entrance to the hut, with gold chains around his feet and a turban full of thorns on his head? Almost every writer provides a different explanation.

Although the subject matter of the pictures inspired by Christ's Passion is the same, the works themselves are rather dissimilar. What distinguishes the *Crown of Thorns* at the National Gallery in London from that of the Prado is not only the number of torturers (four in the former, five in the latter), but also their expression. In the Madrid panel, the cruel bestiality that animates their faces is expressed in the most open manner, although two faces have a look of sly curiosity. In this work, however, the characters appear less monumental than they do in the former.

If we consider *Christ Carrying the Cross,* we find in Vienna (Kunsthistorisches Museum), in Lisbon (on the outer sides of the panels of the *Temptation of Saint Anthony),* and in Madrid (the Royal Palace), clearly narrative interpretations. A procession moves forward in a landscape, and in the first two pictures there are many small characters.

The last version of the theme, which the artist must have done late in his life (Museum of Fine Arts, Ghent), is very different. Seeking an expression that would be even more concentrated than that of the *Crowning with Thorns,* in which the figures are portrayed half-length, Bosch decided to rely totally here on faces seen in close-up, which are more simplified, more striking, and more expressionistic than ever. As he depicts no less than eighteen, he disposes them in such a way that an ensemble of curves is born that articulates the composition. The rest of the composition is supported by two diagonals, one of which is visibly outlined by an arm of the Cross, while the other is less obvious because it is suggested only by the bowed head of Christ and of its imprint on Veronica's veil.

Although He is placed in the center of the

composition, Christ—His face radiant with gentleness—seems remote from his torturers: His eyes are closed and he has an absent look. A similar gentleness can be seen on Veronica's face; her eyelids are also closed; she is alone, stretching forth her precious veil, her soul illumined by the gesture she has just made. Except for the good thief whose expression is pitiful, all the other characters have repugnant faces. Whether their mouths are crying or grimacing, their expressions translate a deep-seated hatred, harsh, vicious contempt, cold cruelty, brutal stupidity, aggressive madness. These feelings are expressed in a manner that is all the more powerful in that Bosch drew the figures with as much acuity as insistence. What is more, he emphasized the volumes so vigorously that they look like sculptures in wood. Nonetheless, he remains a painter, as the refinement of certain colors proves, as well as the harmonious distribution of blues and reds, browns and grays. In short, this is not only one of the most striking pictures that Bosch painted but also one of the most original works that this theme has ever inspired an artist to produce.

I said earlier that Bosch wished to warn his time of the dangers it was running by yielding to the temptations of the devil. Finally, Bosch does more than that: the importance he gives the devil reduces that of the religious characters; sinfulness outweighs devotion. Bosch directs our eyes toward the earth rather than toward heaven. At the same time as he concerns himself with the salvation of souls, he pays much more attention than his predecessors to the everyday behavior of men in the real world. Still, it would be a mistake to think of him as a Renaissance humanist. For Bosch, man is guided neither by his reason nor by his "higher interest." He obeys his instincts; it is the dark side of his being that determines his actions and controls his destiny. In the last analysis, there is considerable uneasiness in Bosch's work, not only in the scenes in which humanity confronts demons and monsters, but also in those in which it gives itself up to pleasure. How many anxious, questioning looks do we discover even in the *Garden of Earthly Delights?* In vain does the painter's faith remain intact, for his spirit as a moralist is disillusioned. His art is one of protest, not of edification.

We have seen that the demons and monsters in his work are invested with an extraordinary verisimilitude. This trait must be emphasized because, in giving them that natural appearance which we find so striking (and which they do not possess to the same degree in the work of his predecessors), Bosch necessarily takes his distances from all the literary models that may be imputed to him. Verbal descriptions always imply a certain vagueness, and our imagination fills in what the words suggest. In Bosch's work, the monsters have well-defined shapes that it is not necessary for us to complete. The world of the imaginary and the non-existent is given a reality that is not only clear but also convincing. The most bizarre peculiarities seem to be completely normal; at once we accept them as possible. Few artists have been able to make us see both the fantastic and the ordinary, the unusual and the familiar, with such intensity and ease. This is because Bosch succeeds to the highest degree in "putting," as Odilon Redon said, "the logic of the visible at the service of the invisible."

It also should be noted that his art, which accords the irrational such a large role, has

nothing delirious about it. The draftsman-
ship may be more or less firm, may be hasty
or even awkward, but it is never the product
of a wandering hand. Nor are the colors
placed by chance; the composition expresses
a will to articulate, to create rhythms, to
achieve balance, to emphasize one detail at
the expense of another. In other words, this
visionary, this narrator, this precursor of the
Surrealists and the Expressionists, this man
who impassions the connoisseurs of esoteric
symbols, never ceases being a painter. The
role that his subject matter plays in his pictures, the difficulties inherent in their
iconographic interpretation, should not make
us forget that finally the value of his work
depends on its artistic qualities. In front of his
Garden of Earthly Delights, we could almost talk
about pure painting, so free is his inventive
use of colors and forms, so eloquent is their
disposition. In sum, the imagination of
Hieronymus Bosch is manifested not only in
his themes but also in his manner. And if on
the one hand his work presents us with disconcerting problems, on the other it offers us
artistic realities that fill us with emotion and
wonder.

LIST OF PLATES

PLATES

1
The Cure of Folly,
c. 1480

2
The Cure of Folly,
c. 1480

3
The Conjurer,
c. 1480

4
The Conjurer (detail),
c. 1480

5
The Ship of Fools (detail),
c. 1480

6
The Ship of Fools (ensemble),
c. 1480

7
The Hawker,
c. 1510

8
The Hay Wain,
triptych (detail panels closed),
c. 1500-1502
The Path of Life

11
The Hay Wain,
triptych (detail center panel), c. 1500-1502
The Struggle for Life

12
The Hay Wain,
triptych (detail center panel), c. 1500-1502
Death

13
The Hay Wain,
triptych (detail center panel),
c. 1500-1502

14
The Hay Wain,
triptych (detail),
c. 1500-1502

15
The Hay Wain,
triptych (detail center panel), c. 1500-1502
Satan Inhabits the World

16
The Hay Wain,
triptych (detail right panel), c. 1500-1502
Hell

17
The Hay Wain,
triptych (detail right panel), c. 1500-1502
Hell

18
The Flood, triptych, c. 1500-1504
The Devil in the Country

19
Scene from Last Judgment, (detail),
c. 1500-1504

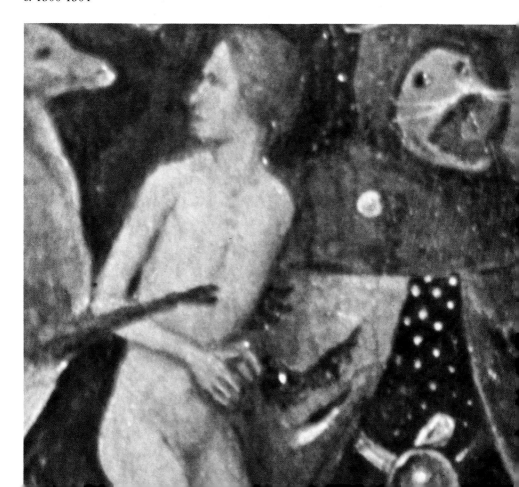

20
The Seven Deadly Sins,
c. 1475

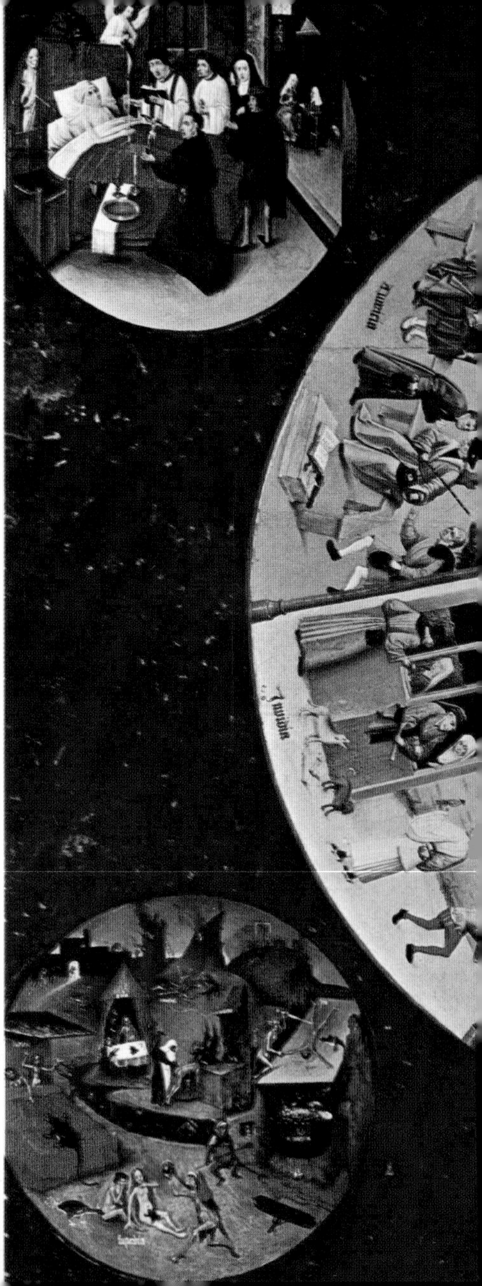

21
The Seven Deadly Sins, (detail),
c. 1475
Pride

22
The Seven Deadly Sins, (detail),
c. 1475
Greed

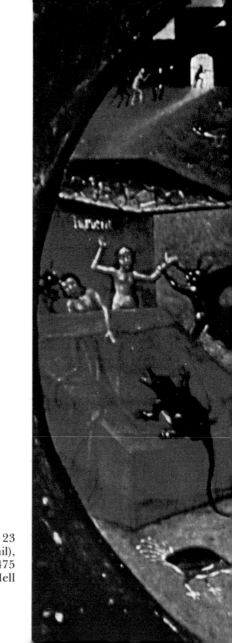

23
The Seven Deadly Sins, (detail),
c. 1475
Hell

24
St. James of Compostela and St. Bavon,
(panels closed),
c. 1480

25
The Last Judgment,
triptych (panels open),
c. 1480

27
The Last Judgment,
triptych (detail center panel),
c. .480

28
The Last Judgment,
triptych (detail center panel),
c. .480

29
The Last Judgment,
triptych (detail center panel),
c. 1480

30
The Last Judgment,
triptych (detail center panel), c. 1480
The Monster with a Basket

31
The Last Judgment,
triptych (detail right panel),
c. 1480

32
The Last Judgment,
triptych (detail center panel),
c. 1480

33
The Last Judgment,
triptych (detail center panel),
c. 1480

34
The Last Judgment,
triptych (detail center panel),
c. 1480

35
The Last Judgment,
triptych (detail center panel),
c. 1480

36
The Garden of Earthly Delights,
triptych (detail left panel), c. 1500
Paradise

37
The Garden of Earthly Delights,
triptych (detail right panel), c. 1500
Musical Hell

38
The Garden of Earthly Delights,
triptych (detail center panel), c. 1500
The Bathing Pool

39
The Garden of Earthly Delights,
triptych (detail center panel), c. 1500
The Young Girls

The Garden of Earthly Delights,
triptych (panels closed), c. 1500
The Creation of the World

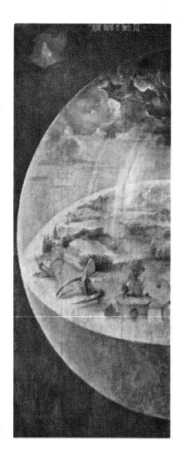

42
The Garden of Earthly Delights,
triptych (detail left panel),
c. 1500

43
The Garden of Earthly Delights,
triptych (detail left panel),
c. 1500

The Garden of Earthly Delights,
triptych (detail right panel),
c. 1500

45
The Garden of Earthly Delights,
triptych (detail right panel),
c. 1500

46
The Garden of Earthly Delights,
triptych (detail center panel),
c. 1500

47
The Garden of Earthly Delights,
triptych (detail center panel),
c. 1500

48
The Garden of Earthly Delights,
triptych (detail upper center panel),
c. 1500

49-50
The Epiphany, triptych (panels open),
c. 1510

51-52
The Epiphany,
triptych (detail center and right panel),
c. 1510

53
The Epiphany,
triptych (detail center panel), c. 1510
Gaspard

54
The Epiphany,
triptych (detail center panel), c. 1510
The Evil Shepherds

55
The Epiphany,
triptych (detail center panel), c. 1510
The Town

56
The Epiphany,
triptych (detail center panel), 1510
The Hordes

57
The Marriage at Cana,
c. 1475-1480

58
Ecce Homo,
c. 1480-1485

59-60
The Crowning with Thorns
(ensemble and detail),
c. 1508

62
Christ Bearing the Cross,
c. 1505

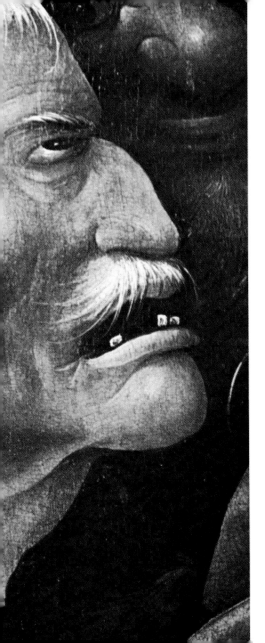

63
Christ Bearing the Cross, (detail),
c. 1505
St. Veronica

64
The Garden of Earthly Delights (left panel),
c. 1500
Garden of Eden (detail)

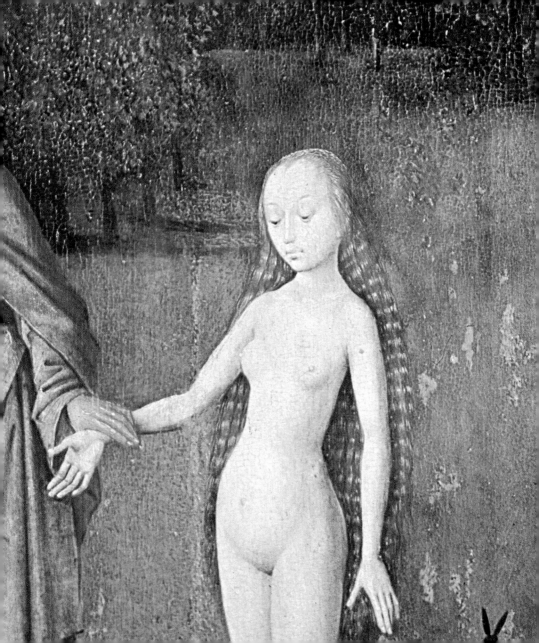

65
The Flood, triptych (detail),
c. 1500-1504
The Evil World

66
The Temptation of St. Anthony,
triptych (detail center panel),
c. 1500
The Procession of Supplicants

67
The Temptation of St. Anthony,
triptych (center panel), c. 1500
The Black Mass (detail)

68
The Temptation of St. Anthony,
triptych (center panel), c. 1500
The Alchemical Child (detail)

69
The Temptation of St. Anthony,
triptych (detail left panel), c. 1500
The Man Rooted in Sin

70
The Temptation of St. Anthony,
triptych (detail left panel) c. .500
The Heretics

71
The Arrest of Christ,
triptych (panels closed),
c. 1500

72
The Temptation of St. Anthony,
triptych, (panels open),
c. 1500

The Temptation of St. Anthony,
triptych, (detail right panel), c. 1500
The Town

74
The Temptation of St. Anthony,
triptych, (detail right panel), c. 1500
The Town

75
The Temptation of St. Anthony,
triptych (detail left panel),
c. 1500

76
The Temptation of St. Anthony,
triptych (detail left panel),
c. 1500

77
The Temptation of St. Anthony,
triptych (detail center panel),
c. 1500

78
The Temptation of St. Anthony,
triptych,
c. 1500

79
The Temptation of St. Anthony,
triptych,
c. 1500

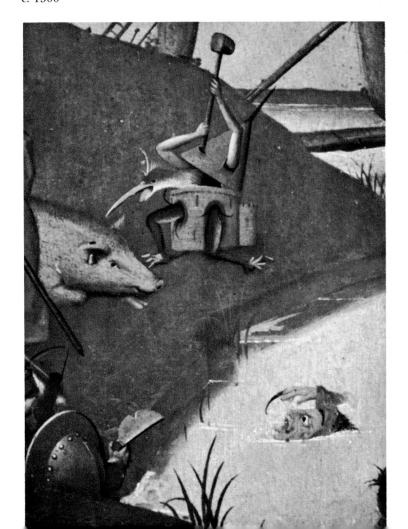

80
St. Jerome in Prayer,
c. 1505

81
St. John the Baptist in the Desert,
c. 1504

82
St. Jerome in Prayer, (detail),
c. 1505

83
St. John the Baptist in the Desert, (detail)
c. 1504

84
St. John the Evangelist in Patmos,
c. 1504